Languages of the World

Urdu

Lucia Raatma
Naresh Sharma

Raintree

www.raintreepublishers.co.uk
Visit our website to find out
more information about
Raintree books.

To order:
☎ Phone 0845 6044371
📄 Fax +44 (0) 1865 312263
📠 Email myorders@raintreepublishers.co.uk

Customers from outside the UK please telephone +44 1865 312262

Raintree is an imprint of Capstone Global Library Limited,
a company incorporated in England and Wales having its
registered office at 7 Pilgrim Street, London, EC4V 6LB –
Registered company number: 6695582

Edited by Dan Nunn, Rebecca Rissman, and Catherine Veitch
Designed by Marcus Bell
Picture research by Ruth Blair
Originated by Capstone Global Library
Printed and bound in China by South China Printing
  Company Ltd

ISBN 978 1 4062 2451 1
15 14 13 12 11
10 9 8 7 6 5 4 3 2 1

British Library Cataloguing in Publication Data
Raatma, Lucia.
Sharma, Naresh
Urdu. -- (Languages of the world)
491.4'39-dc22
A full catalogue record for this book is available from the
British Library.

Acknowledgements
We would like to thank the following for permission to
reproduce photographs: Alamy pp. 6 (© Jon Parker Lee), 10
(© Picture Contact BV), 14 (© MBI), 22 (© Idris Ahmed),
29 (© Neil McAllister); Corbis pp. 9 (© Steve Hix/Somos
Images), 12 (© epa), 19 (© Annie Griffiths Belt), 20 (© Galen
Rowell), 23 (© Jonathan Blair), 26 (© Matiullah Achakzai/epa);
iStockphoto pp. 15 (© Pathathai Chungyam); Photolibrary p.
18 (Bill Stevenson); Shutterstock pp. 5 (© Asianet-Pakistan), 7
(© afaizal), 8 (© aspen rock), 11 (© Marilyn Barbone), 13 (©
michaeljung), 15, 21 (© ansar80), 17 (© Arvind Balaraman), 24
(© zeber), 25 (© JeremyRichards), 27 (© Eva Gruendemann),
28 (© JeremyRichards).

Cover photograph of Indian boy reproduced with permission
of Shutterstock (© Rohit Seth).

We would like to thank Naresh Sharma for his invaluable help
in the preparation of this book.

Every effort has been made to contact copyright holders
of material reproduced in this book. Any omissions will
be rectified in subsequent printings if notice is given to
the publisher.

Contents

Urdu around the world 4

Who speaks Urdu? 6

Urdu and English 8

Learning Urdu 10

Saying hello and goodbye 12

Talking about yourself 14

Asking about others 16

At home 18

Family life 20

At school 22

Sport 24

Food and drink 26

Clothes and shopping 28

Pronunciation guide 30

Find out more 32

Index 32

Urdu words are in italics, *like this*. You can find out how to say them by looking in the pronunciation guide.

Urdu around the world

The Urdu language is spoken all over the world. It is one of the main languages of Pakistan. Urdu is also one of the languages of India. Pakistan and India are both in Asia.

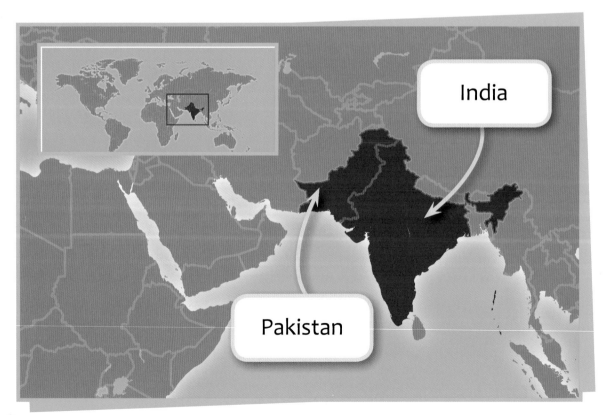

India

Pakistan

Many people in Pakistan speak Urdu.

People in many other countries speak Urdu, too. Urdu speakers can be found in Afghanistan, Australia, South Africa, the United States, Germany, the United Kingdom, and other places.

Who speaks Urdu?

Throughout the world there are about 100 million Urdu speakers. Around 400,000 of those live in the United Kingdom. The United States is home to more than 250,000 Urdu speakers.

Urdu is spoken by many people in the United Kingdom.

In Saudi Arabia, thousands of people speak Urdu.

In India, almost 50 million people speak Urdu. Around 11 million Urdu speakers live in Pakistan. Saudi Arabia has many thousands of Urdu speakers, too.

Urdu and English

You may already know some Urdu words. Some of them have become part of the English language. For example, *khaki* comes from the Urdu language. It means "dust-coloured".

Khakis are named after a colour in the Urdu language.

"Pyjamas" is a word that came from the Urdu word *pājāmā*.

The English word "pyjamas" comes from the Urdu word *pājāmā*. If something is easy or soft, we might say it's cushy. That comes from the Urdu word *khushī*, which means happiness.

Learning Urdu

The Urdu alphabet is very different from the alphabet used to write English. It is read from right to left. There are 39 basic letters, and 13 extra ones.

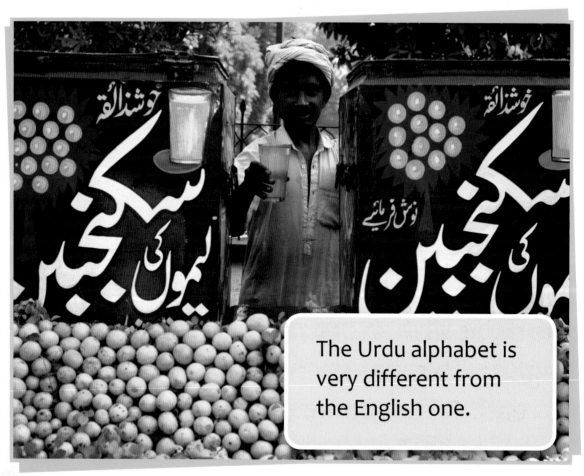

The Urdu alphabet is very different from the English one.

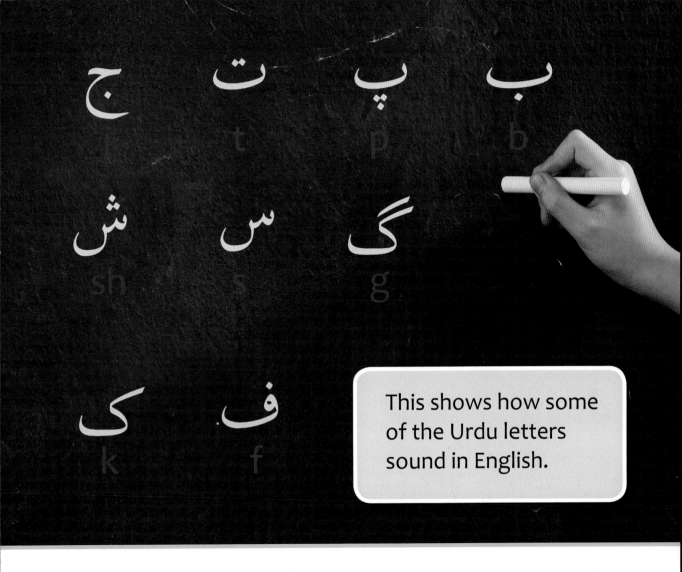

ب b
پ p
ت t
ج j
گ g
س s
ش sh
ف f
ک k

This shows how some of the Urdu letters sound in English.

In this book Urdu words are written in the same alphabet that is used to write English. This makes them easier for you to read. The extra marks on some of the letters show how the words should sound.

Saying hello and goodbye

In Pakistan, men may shake hands with each other when they meet. If they know each other well, they may hug. Women often hug and kiss when they meet.

An Urdu speaker might say "*assalām ālekum*" ("hello") or "*subha bākhair*" ("good morning"). Later, he might say "*shab bākhair*" ("goodnight") and "*khudā hāfiz*" ("goodbye").

Talking about yourself

When you meet someone new you might say "*Āp se milkar khushī huī*" ("Pleased to meet you"). Then you might say "*Merā nām Lucia hai*" ("My name is Lucia").

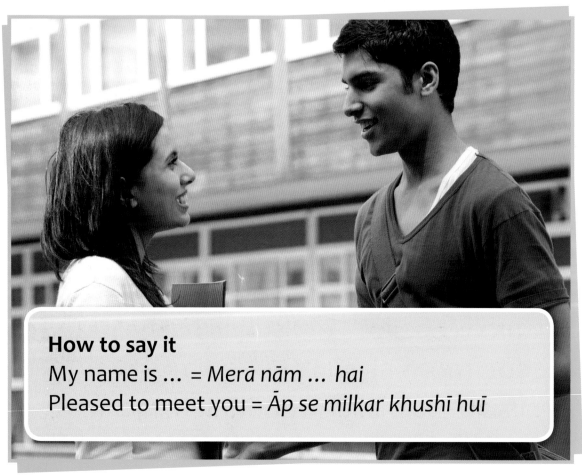

How to say it
My name is ... = *Merā nām ... hai*
Pleased to meet you = *Āp se milkar khushī huī*

How to say it
Sorry = *māf karnā*
I am from . . .
= *Maĩ . . . se hũ*

You might also tell someone where you are from by saying "*Maĩ Pakistan se hũ*" ("I am from Pakistan"). If you make a mistake you might say "*māf karnā*" ("sorry").

Asking about others

When greeting someone, you might say *"khush āmdīd"* ("welcome"). Then you might ask *"Āpkā nām kyā hai?"* ("What is your name?") and *"Āp kahā̃ se haĩ?"* ("Where are you from?")

How to say it

What is your name? = *Āpkā nām kyā hai?*

Where are you from? = *Āp kahā̃ se haĩ?*

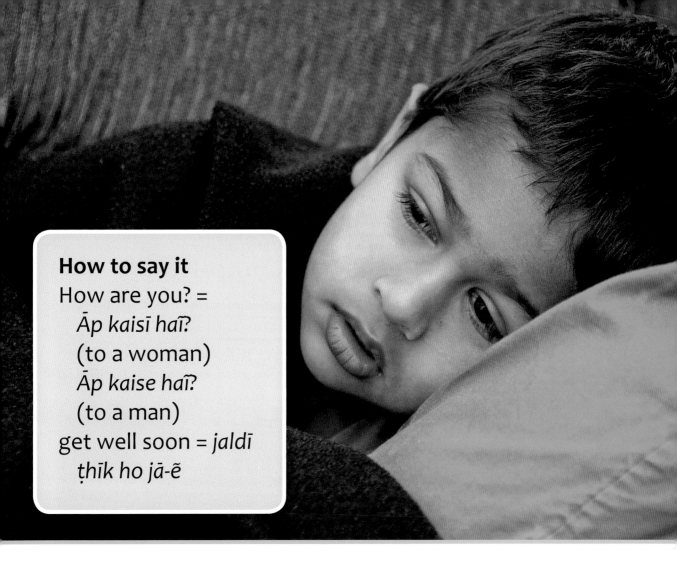

How to say it

How are you? =
  Āp kaisī haĩ?
  (to a woman)
  Āp kaise haĩ?
  (to a man)
get well soon = *jaldī
  ṭhīk ho jā-ẽ*

To say "How are you?" you would ask a woman, "*Āp kaisī haĩ?*" For a man, you would ask "*Āp kaise haĩ?*" If someone is ill, you might say "*jaldī ṭhīk ho jā-ẽ*" ("get well soon")

At home

Some people in Pakistan live in big cities. They make their homes in apartment buildings or flats. They have modern things like televisions and computers.

How to say it
city = *shehar*
building = *imārat*
street = *rāstā*

How to say it
home = *ghar*
door = *darwāzā*
window = *khiṛkī*

Other people in Pakistan live in villages.
Some homes are made of mud or clay.
They might have dirt floors. These
homes might not have electricity.

Family life

In Pakistan one house can be home to an older couple with their sons, sons' wives, unmarried daughters, and grandchildren. Most daughters live with their parents until they get married.

How to say it
father = *wālid*
mother = *wālidā*
children = *bache*

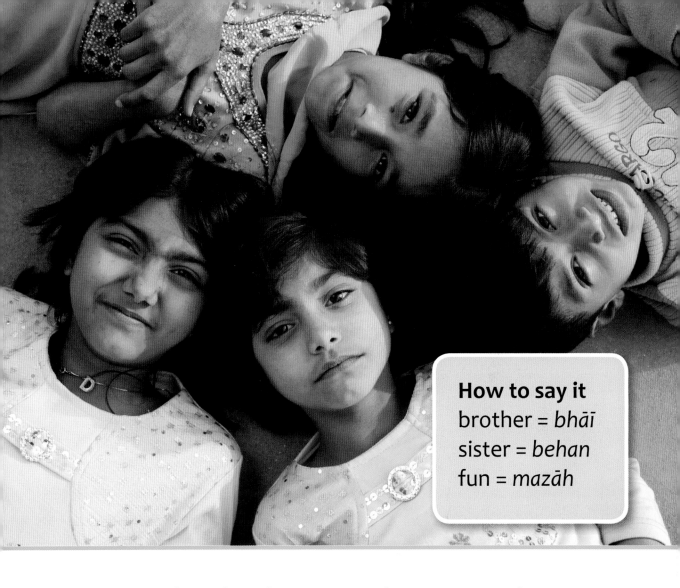

How to say it
brother = *bhāī*
sister = *behan*
fun = *mazāh*

Boys and girls play together. But when they get older, women do not usually mix with men from outside their family. Sometimes men and women sit in separate areas of restaurants.

At school

Many children in Pakistan go to school, but most pupils are boys. Throughout the country many people cannot read. The government (people who run the country) is trying to change that.

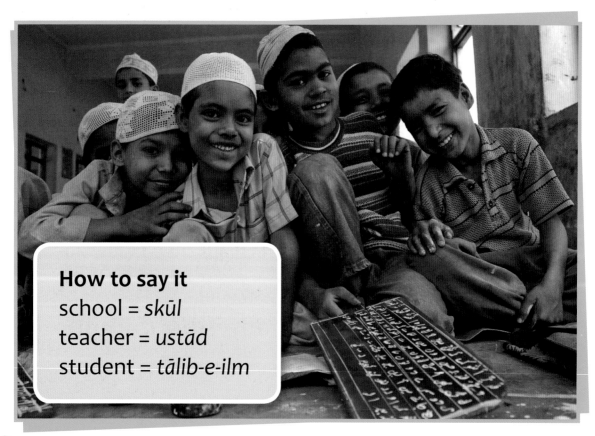

How to say it
school = *skūl*
teacher = *ustād*
student = *tālib-e-ilm*

Pupils at schools in Pakistan study
mathematics, history, science,
and English. They also learn about
religion.

Sport

Cricket is the main sport of Pakistan. This game is played with bats and balls. People in Pakistan also like to play hockey, squash, and football.

How to say it
ball = *gend*
run = *dauṛnā*
shoe = *jūtā*

How to say it
game = *khel*
horse = *ghoṛā*
hat = *ṭopī*

Some people in Pakistan play polo. There are two teams. Players ride horses and hit a ball into the other team's goal. A famous polo tournament is held in Pakistan each year.

Food and drink

Many people in Pakistan eat beef, chicken, and vegetables. *Dāl* is a popular lentil stew. Most meals also include a flat bread called *chapātī*.

How to say it
meat = *gosht*
chicken = *murghī*
lentil stew = *dāl*
flat bread = *chapātī*

How to say it
yogurt drink = *lassī*
tea = *chāi*

Lassī is a delicious drink made from yogurt. Many people also drink *chāi*, which is a kind of tea. *Khīr* is a rice pudding made with nuts.

Clothes and shopping

In Pakistan clothing is often brightly coloured. Both men and women wear outfits called *salwar kamīz*. Women may also wear a scarf called a *dupatta*.

How to say it
dress = *libās*
shirt = *kamīz*
trousers = *patlūn*

How to say it
fruit = *phal*
vegetable = *sabzī*

People in Pakistan often shop in an outdoor market called a *bāzār*. They buy fresh fruit and vegetables. They may also buy rugs and blankets. Pakistan is also known for its pottery.

Pronunciation guide

English	Urdu	Pronunciation
ball	*gend*	*gend*
book	*kitāb*	*kitaab*
brother	*bhāī*	*bhaa-ee*
building	*imārat*	*imaarat*
chicken	*murghī*	*murghee*
children	*bache*	*bachay*
city	*shehar*	*shehar*
door	*darwāzā*	*darwaazaa*
dress	*libās*	*libaas*
English	*angrezī*	*angrezee*
father	*wālid*	*waalid*
flat bread	*chapātī*	*chapaatee*
fruit	*phal*	*phal*
fun	*mazāh*	*mazaah*
game	*khel*	*khayl*
get well soon	*jaldī ṭhīk ho jā-ē*	*jaldee theek ho jaa-ay*
goodbye	*khudā hāfiz*	*khudaa haafiz*
good morning	*subha bākhair*	*subha baakhair*
goodnight	*shab bākhair*	*shab baakhair*
happiness	*khushī*	*khushee*
hat	*ṭopī*	*topee*
hello	*assalām ālekum*	*assalaam aalaykum*
history	*tārīkh*	*taareekh*
home	*ghar*	*ghar*
horse	*ghoṛā*	*ghoraa*

How are you?	Āp kaisī haĩ? (female)	Aa
	Āp kaise haĩ? (male)	Aa
I am from ...	Maĩ ... se hū̃	Ma
lentil stew	dāl	daa
market	bāzār	baa
meat	gosht	gosh
mother	wālidā	waal
My name is ...	Merā nām ... hai	Mera
Pleased to meet you	Āp se milkar khushī huī	Aap s
		huee
pyjamas	pājāmā	paajaam
rice pudding	khīr	kheer
run	daurnā	daurnaa
school	skūl	school
shirt	kamīz	kameez
shoe	jūtā	jootaa
sister	behan	behan
sorry	māf karnā	maaf karnaa
street	rāstā	raastaa
student	tālib-e-ilm	taalib-e-ilm
tea	chāi	chaai
teacher	ustād	ustaad
trousers	patlūn	patloon
vegetable	sabzī	sabzee
welcome	khush āmdīd	khush aamdeed
What is your name?	Āpkā nām kyā hai?	Aapkaa naam kyaa hai?
Where are you from?	Āp kahā̃ se haĩ?	Aap kahaa say hai?
window	khiṛkī	khirkee
yogurt drink	lassī	lassee

...ter and Connie Roop

...ary, 2008)

...P is for Pakistan, Shazia Razzak

...Children's Books, 2007)

...or parents and teachers

...he following as a guide to pronunciation:

...ound, as in the "n" in hunger

..." sound, pronounced by the tongue touching the back

...e upper teeth

...' as in train

...oft "d" sound, pronounced by the tongue touching the back of the upper teeth

r = the Urdu "r" sound is rolled more than the English "r" sound

ṛ = similar sound to "r", but the tongue flaps against the roof of the mouth. At first it can be tricky to pronounce it.

Index

alphabet 10, 11

clothing 28

food 26

home 18, 19, 20

language 4

meeting 12, 14

school 22, 23

sport 24